The Many Lives of Benjamin Franklin

Written down and illustrated by Aliki

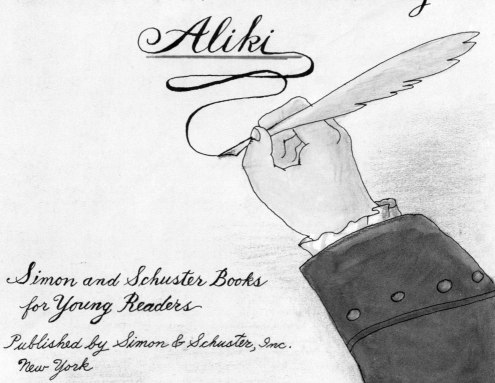

Simon and Schuster Books
for Young Readers

Published by Simon & Schuster, Inc.
New York

Copyright © 1977, 1988 by Aliki Brandenburg. All rights reserved including the right of reproduction in
whole or in part in any form. Published by Simon and Schuster Books for Young Readers, a Division of
Simon & Schuster, Inc., Simon & Schuster Building, Rockefeller Center, 1230 Avenue of the Americas,
New York 10020. SIMON AND SCHUSTER BOOKS FOR YOUNG READERS is a trademark of
Simon & Schuster, Inc. SIMON & SCHUSTER and colophon are registered trademarks of Simon &
Schuster, Inc.

10 9 8 7 6 5 4 3
10 9 8 7 6 5   (pbk.)

Library of Congress Cataloging in Publication Data
Aliki.
    The many lives of Benjamin Franklin/written down and illustrated by Aliki.
    Summary: Recounts the story of Benjamin Franklin's life and his many activities and achievements.
    1. Franklin, Benjamin, 1706-1790—Juvenile literature. 2. Statesmen—United States—Biography—
Juvenile literature. 3. Printers—United States—Biography—Juvenile literature. [1. Franklin, Benjamin,
1706-1790. 2. Statesmen.] I. Title.
E302.6.F8A48 1988   973.3′092′4—dc19
[B]   [92]   87-22872
ISBN 0-671-66119-1
ISBN 0-671-66491-3 (pbk.)

For Carolyn W. Field

The Free Library of Philadelphia - founded by Benjamin Franklin in 1731.

These are some of the 17 children of Josiah and Abiah Franklin. Ben was the tenth and youngest son.

'Tis a good thing the table is big.

JOSIAH FRANKLIN SOAP AND CANDLEMAKER

You can do this work when you grow up.

I don't like the smell.

Ben taught himself to read before anyone even noticed.

The house on Milk Street where Ben was born.

Benjamin Franklin was born with just one life.
But as he grew, his curiosity, his sense of humor,
  and his brilliant mind, turned him into a man
  with many lives.

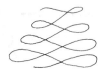

Benjamin Franklin was born in Boston in 1706.
His mother and his father, who was a candlemaker,
  had many children.
But they saw Ben was special.
He was curious. He loved books.
And even as a child, he was full of bright ideas.

Ben was always thinking—even at play.
He liked to swim, and tried different ways.
Once he made paddles so he could go faster.

Ben's paddles were wooden, with a hole for his thumb. He made paddles for his feet, too.

Another time, when he was flying his kite
    near a pond, he had another idea.
He went for a swim holding on to the kite string.
Just as he thought, the kite pulled him
    across the water.

Ben felt like taking a swim.

He tied his kite to a branch.

Then he had an idea.

He let the kite pull him across the pond, and his friend carried his clothes to the other side.

Ben loved school, but his parents did not have
the money for him to continue.
After only two years, he had to leave and choose
a trade.
It was decided that Ben would learn to be a printer
like his brother, James.
So when he was twelve, Ben was sent to live with him.

Ben's job as an apprentice was to clean and sort type, sweep the floor, and sell newspapers.

Ben spent nights and Sundays reading and practicing his writing.

Ben learned quickly.
He worked long, hard hours.
Still, he found time to read every book he could
    borrow, and saved the money he earned
    to buy more.

At the shop, Ben wanted to do more than
   just help print his brother's newspaper.
He wanted to write in it, too.
So he thought of a way.

James began finding mysterious letters under
   the office door.
They were signed "Silence Dogood."
Silence wrote such funny stories, clever essays
   and poetry, James printed them.
In fact, they helped him sell more newspapers.
Little did he know that Silence Dogood
   was his little brother Ben.

Silence Dogood wrote that she was a poor widow with some ideas she wished to share.

She said she would write again.

James showed the letters to his friends.

I don't know who she is but I'll print them.

Clever!

Interesting!

Funny!

Another letter!

People could hardly wait for Widow Dogood's next letter.

Ben wrote more and more letters.

But when James found out, he was angry. Ben was not allowed to write any more.

He decided to go somewhere else, where he could write. So when he was 17, he left James and Boston.

Ben went to Philadelphia to start a life of his own. He found a job with a printer. He read and collected more books. He worked and saved until at last he bought his own shop. Now he could print his own newspaper and all the letters he wished.

Philadelphia 1723

B. FRANKLIN

PRINTER
STATIONER

PENNSYLVANIA
GAZETTE

LEGAL BLANKS

Ben worked very hard and even delivered his packages himself.

A few years later, Ben met and married a young girl
    named Deborah Read.
Deborah worked hard, too.
She managed their new house, and her own general
    store next to Ben's print shop.
Before long they had two children to help them.

Ben's father made soap and candles for Deborah to sell.

WILLIAM was the oldest.

FRANCIS was born in 1732. When he was four, he got very sick and died.

Baby SARAH was called "Sally" by her father.

Ben's newspaper was a great success.

Then he began printing a yearly calendar called Poor
    Richard's Almanack.

The booklet was full of advice, news, and information.

What made it even more special were the wise,
    witty sayings of Poor Richard.

Year after year, people bought the almanac.

It made Ben famous.

Benjamin Franklin pretended Richard Saunders wrote the almanac.

1733
Poor Richard's
ALMANACK

"Poor Richard" was
Richard Saunders, a poor
astrologer who liked to spend
his time gazing at the stars.
His wife nagged him to get
to work and make some money,
so he decided to please her.
That is why he wrote his almanac.

SUNRISE   SUNSET

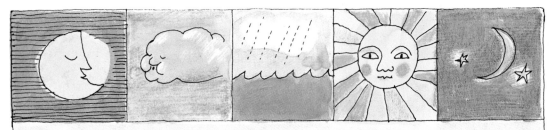

The almanac gave weather forecasts, tide changes, astrology news,

the right time to plant, sow, and harvest,
recipes, cures for ailments, ideas, inventions, news events and

Poor Richard's Sayings:

Early to bed and early to rise, makes a man healthy, wealthy, and wise.

Beware of little expenses. A small leak will sink a great ship.

'Tis hard for an empty bag to stand upright.

Up, sluggard, and waste not life. In the grave will be sleeping enough.

A word to the wise is enough.

At the working man's house, hunger looks in but dares not enter.

Every little makes a mickle.

One today is worth two tomorrows.

Meanwhile, Benjamin Franklin was busy living
  other lives.
He loved Philadelphia.
It was a new city full of promise, and Benjamin
  was there at the right time.
He started a club called the Junto, where friends met
  to discuss books and ideas.

Men from many trades came to the weekly Junto meetings.

He lent out his books, and soon others did the same.
This began the first free lending library in America.
He found new ways to light the streets, and to have
    them cleaned and paved, too.
He started a police force, a fire department,
    a hospital, and an Academy.
He helped make laws.
Philadelphia became as famous as Benjamin Franklin.

Benjamin Franklin in his fireman's helmet.

A lamplighter walked through the streets at dusk lighting lamps.

By the time he was forty-two, Benjamin Franklin
had enough money from his printing to live
in comfort with his family.
He gave up the shop to spend all his time
with his ideas.
A new life began.

Ben started scientific experiments, and soon
became a master.
He was the first to prove lightning was electricity.
One day, during a thunderstorm, he tried a dangerous
experiment with a kite and a key, and found
he was right.
He realized how to protect houses from lightning,
and invented the lightning rod.

People put "Franklin Rods" up on their rooftops in America
and in other countries, too.

Benjamin Franklin's Dangerous Kite Experiment

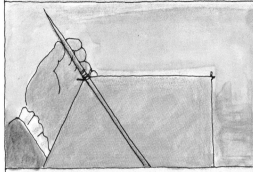

He attached a pointed metal rod to the kite.

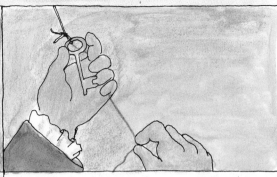

He tied a silk cord to the kite string and a key to the cord.

He and his son, William, took shelter. Lightning struck the rod.

He touched the wet key and felt a shock. Electricity had traveled down the kite string to the key. The silk cord stopped it from going further.

He invented the Franklin stove.
It fit into a fireplace and could
heat a whole house. The stoves
are used even today.

He found safer routes
for ships to travel.

He became Postmaster General
and found safer ways to send mail.

He designed a chair-table.

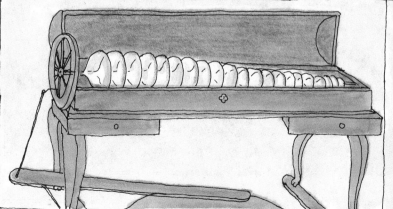

He made a musical
instrument called
an Armonica.

It was played
by rubbing wet
fingers against
glass discs.

Famous composers
wrote music
for it.

He experimented in his garden and found better ways to grow crops.

He invented glasses called bifocals. He could see far, out of the top of the glasses, and near, out of the bottom.

He introduced Swiss barley, Chinese rhubarb, Newton apples, willow for baskets, and turnips to America.

He found out that black cloth keeps one warmer than white by laying pieces of cloth in the snow. After some time, the black cloth was warmed by the sun and sank into the snow. The white didn't.

Benjamin Franklin made many discoveries in his
   lifetime, but he refused money for them.
He said his ideas belonged to everyone.
He wrote them down and they were translated
   into many languages.
He became the best known man in America.

More than anything, Benjamin hoped people would
    listen to his most important idea—
    freedom for his country.
For at that time, America was an English colony.
He—and others—did not want to be ruled by England
    any longer.

He was sent to England to seek independence
    for his country.
For eighteen long years, Benjamin stayed
    there and worked for that goal.
In 1775, he returned to Philadelphia,
    sad and disappointed.
His wife had died. War with England had begun,
    and America was still not free.

Benjamin and his friends discussed ways to gain freedom for America.

He and William left for England. He made many trips back to Philadelphia to visit Deborah and Sally. Deborah did not go with Benjamin because she was afraid of the long dangerous voyage.

Pennsylvania State House, now called Independence Hall, in 1776.

Benjamin Franklin, Thomas Jefferson, John Adams, John Hancock, and 52 others, signed the Declaration of Independence in Philadelphia on July 4, 1776.

Yet he persisted.

Benjamin Franklin and other great Americans
helped Thomas Jefferson write
the Declaration of Independence.

They were determined to be free.

But they knew they would first have to fight
a long, terrible war.

And they did.

General George Washington led many battles during the
Revolutionary War.

In France, he visited King Louis XVI and Queen Marie Antoinette. Though everyone wore fancy clothes and powdered wigs, Benjamin Franklin did not. Everyone was impressed with the inventor's plain clothes and simple ways.

But they needed help.
Benjamin Franklin was old and weary when again
    he sailed away.
This time he went to ask for aid from the King of
    France.

Benjamin was greeted as a hero.
People in France knew about him and his inventions,
    and they loved him.
Finally, the King agreed.
With his help, the war with England was won.
America was free at last.

In 1781 the war ended. The Liberty Bell in Independence Hall rang out.

On September 13, 1785, his ship entered Philadelphia Harbor. Bells rang, cannons boomed, and hundreds of people waited to welcome Benjamin home.

He was reunited at last with his daughter Sally, her husband Richard Bache, and his grandchildren.

Benjamin Franklin had served abroad long enough.
He wanted to spend his last years at home.
When he finally returned from France, it was 1785.
He thought he had been forgotten.

But he was not forgotten.
He was greeted with wild celebrations.
He saw his country still needed him.
He became the first governor of Pennsylvania and
    helped write the Constitution of the United States.

On September 17, 1787, Benjamin Franklin and the other great writers of the Constitution signed the document on which all laws of the United States are based.

Benjamin Franklin lived eighty-four years.
He left the world his inventions, his ideas,
  his wisdom and his wit.
He lived his many lives for us all.